KING JAMES I

A Life from Beginning to End

Copyright © 2019 by Hourly History.

Table of Contents

Introduction

James was born at Edinburgh Castle in Scotland on June 19, 1566. Just one year later, he was crowned King James VI of Scotland after his father was murdered and his mother imprisoned. At the age of 37, he would go on to claim the throne of England and Ireland as well, reigning the kingdoms as James I.

Perhaps James' greatest problem was that he achieved his goal of becoming king of both Scotland and England. Instead of uniting two countries and two faiths, he spent a lifetime trying to please both and ended up pleasing neither. The division between Protestants and Catholics began with James' great-grandmother's brother, Henry VIII of England. Henry had denounced Rome and proclaimed himself head of the Church of England, kicking off the Reformation in England. Since that time, both faiths vied for superiority.

This was the chasm inherited at birth by James. He was highly educated and interested in religion, especially as it applied to everyday life. Yet he invariably failed to grasp the abstract differences and goals of the warring factions that demanded his loyalty. Every political decision he made was lamented by his opponents. Eventually James became aloof and uninterested. Instead of taking any action, he ignored the Scottish Kirk and later dissolved the English Parliament. Tragically, he was never able to gain the upper hand with either institution. James could have been an excellent king. Instead of ruling, however, his time was spent avoiding confrontation with his critics.

James died as king of England, Ireland, and Scotland. He failed to unite his countries, who were never more at odds than at the time of his death.

Chapter One

Destined for Greatness

"No more tears. I will now think about revenge."

—Mary, Queen of Scots following the murder of David Rizzio

No king had ever ruled both England and Scotland, but James of Scotland appeared destined to do so at birth. His mother, Mary, Queen of Scots, was the great-granddaughter of Henry VII of England and the grandniece of Henry VIII. James' father, Henry Stuart—more commonly known as Lord Darnley—was also a direct descendant of Henry VII.

At the time of James' birth, Queen Elizabeth I of England was toying with a number of eager suitors without any real intentions of getting married and producing an heir. James of Scotland was in a perfect position to fill the vacancy.

James' mother Mary became Scotland's queen when she was six days old, following the death of her mother, Mary of Guise. Young Mary, however, spent little time in Scotland. She was betrothed to the French dauphin, Francis, and spent her childhood in the glittery world of Versailles being groomed for a brilliant future as queen of France. She showed very little interest in her own country. Mary's future, however, changed abruptly. Her husband, Francis, died while still in adolescence. Shattered, Mary returned to Scotland. It was a world she hardly knew, and she found it dreadful. After years in France, she barely spoke the language. Scotland was a gloomy place compared to France. And after living a cultured existence at Versailles, she considered Scots to be near-barbarians.

But Mary was attractive, young, and ambitious. She had a certain claim on the English throne. When she married Lord Darnley four years after her return to Scotland, his bloodline was the main attraction. Darnley also descended from Henry VII, Henry being Darnley's great-grandfather. By joining forces, Mary hoped to improve her chances of becoming Queen Elizabeth's successor. Both Mary and Darnley were Catholics, but Mary was tolerant of the new religious reform that had swept over Britain.

However, Lord Darnley proved a bad choice, as were so many of Mary's decision. He immediately demanded to be named co-ruler and proclaimed himself king of the Scots. He wanted equal powers. Mary grew to hate her husband. She did become pregnant very quickly after the wedding, but the relationship between husband and wife deteriorated even faster. Mary became close (how close can only be conjectured) to her Italian secretary, David Rizzio, and bestowed on him the powers her husband Darnley craved.

Furious, Darnley spread rumors that the child Mary was carrying might not be his. He then collected a group of trusted men, which included Lord Bothwell and Mary's half-brother, Lord Moray, and, and stormed into Mary's private quarters one evening while she was dining with Rizzio. Rizzio was dragged into an antechamber and stabbed repeatedly. Mary was seven months pregnant at the time.

It was difficult for the culprits to deny their crime. They were literally holding the bloody knives. Nervously, Darnley begged for forgiveness. Not yet secure in her own position, Mary had no choice but to forgive. But she did not forget.

Darnley and his friends quickly took control, effectively placing Mary under house arrest. Darnley blamed the entire episode on Lord Moray, Mary's half-brother, and assured her they were both in danger. He made a production of getting both of them to safety at Dunbar Castle. But Mary's enmity toward Darnley only grew. She was biding her time.

Mary and Darnley's son James was born on June 19, 1566. Mary turned his baptism on December 17 into a grand event. With her ambitions still focused south, on England, she invited all the important noblemen to the celebration. The king of France sent handsome gifts; Elizabeth I was chosen as one of the godparents. Mary made it clear that her son was destined for more than the relative obscurity of Scotland. The baptism was great theater. Hesitantly, Mary allowed the baptism to be a Catholic one, even if that did not sit well with members of the Protestant Scottish Kirk. The only person of note who was absent from the baptism was the baby's father, Lord Darnley. Mary would not permit his presence; they no longer shared a home or a bed.

Rizzio was quickly replaced in Mary's affections, and perhaps her bed, by Lord Bothwell, one of the Rizzio's murderers. It may seem like a strange choice, but perhaps it was not. Darnley's ambitions were becoming dangerous, and having both her half-brother Moray and Bothwell on her side might have appeared most favorable for Mary. If there were any way to dispose of Darnley, Moray promised to support a marriage between Mary and Bothwell.

In February of 1567, both Mary and Darnley were living in Edinburgh; however, Mary and young James were at Holyrood, while Darnley stayed at nearby Kirk o' Field. At two o'clock in the morning, a tremendous explosion could be heard throughout the area. A blast had been ignited at Kirk o' Field below Darnley's room. Darnley was found in the garden, apparently strangled to death.

Bothwell was the clear perpetrator of this vile deed, and it is almost a certainty that Mary was aware of the plot against her husband. However, it remains unclear whether Mary was a willing accomplice or a victim of Bothwell's ambitions. According to some sources, Mary was kidnapped and raped by Bothwell shortly after her husband's murder.

In any case, Bothwell was acquitted of all charges against him, and Moray made good on his promise and arranged a marriage between Mary and Bothwell. At this point, Mary's reputation among her people was in tatters. Too many murders were being associated with her, and Mary's subjects could not fathom that she had chosen to marry the man accused of murdering her previous husband. The mobs jeered her, and the confederate lords placed her in custody at Lochleven Castle. One-year-old James was taken to Stirling Castle and placed under the guardianship of the trusted Lord Mar.

Mary had no choice but to abdicate her throne. She formally did so on July 24, 1567, under the condition that Bothwell was allowed to flee to freedom. On July 29, James was officially crowned in a Protestant ceremony and became James VI of Scotland. He never saw his mother again.

Chapter Two

The Boy King

"I am now sole king."

—James VI following Mary's execution

James VI may have been crowned king of Scotland, but he was a mere child. During his minority, he went through several regents, all of whom attempted to rule Scotland their way. The main goal which they all seemed to agree on was to keep the boy king safe from the various feuding Scottish clans. This would lead to keeping the orphaned king isolated from his subjects and other children at Stirling Castle. James never knew the closeness of a family.

Since his mother, Mary, had been a Catholic, great pains were taken to choose regents with impeccable Protestant credentials. This was absolutely necessary if James were to succeed the devoutly Protestant Elizabeth I. While James was the most likely candidate, he wasn't the only one. His great-grandmother, Henry VIII's sister Margaret Tudor, had been queen of Scotland, and her great-granddaughter Arabella also had a claim to the throne. But Arabella was female, which made her less desirable as an heir. Other possibilities were the descendants of Henry VIII's younger sister, Mary Tudor. But that too wasn't a given.

The Kirk, the powerful Church of Scotland, demanded that James be raised as a proper Protestant according to their rules. While in England the monarch was head of the church, the Scottish Kirk considered itself above secular rule. James would spend much of his life at odds with the Kirk, who considered even Elizabeth I as having "popish ways." The Scottish lords and the members of the Kirk would engage in a long battle over the supremacy of the state versus the supremacy of the church.

Perhaps it was his isolation that made James embrace learning. He was a superb and eager scholar, moving between Scottish, Latin, Greek, and French languages effortlessly. Elizabeth I was pleased with the progress reports she received. One of James' tutors, George Buchanan, had a special influence on the young king that would last throughout his life. Buchanan was a firm believer in citizens' right to rebel against a monarch of the wrong religion. By wrong, of course, he meant Catholic. For James, this was the beginning of trying to please the hardcore Kirk, the more moderate members of his council, and later the British Parliament. It was important that he never become associated with Catholicism. However, James' lifelong attempt to mollify everyone eventually made him a far less effective monarch than he could have been.

In 1579, James' isolation ended abruptly with the arrival of a distant cousin on his father's side, 37-year-old Esmé Stewart, who had been raised in France. Sophisticated, charming, and cultured, Esmé quickly enthralled his lonely, 13-year-old cousin. Their relationship was publicly very affectionate. For the remainder of his life, James would prefer the company of handsome and sophisticated men to women.

Since Esmé was French and Catholic (like James' mother), the Kirk was appalled. This association was unacceptable. Unmindful, James elevated Esmé with powers and riches at court. He himself wasn't Catholic, he insisted. Notwithstanding, the Kirk couldn't accept this association and demanded Esmé's expulsion from

Scotland. James resisted but was unable to fight the power of the Kirk. Esmé was sent back to France in 1582, where he soon died. The chasm between king and Kirk continued to deepen.

The Kirk wasn't the only entity to divide the king's loyalties. While imprisoned in England, his mother, Mary, was surrounded by French Catholic lords who wanted to see her back on the throne. Mary, who hadn't seen her son since he was an infant, greatly resented that he had usurped what she considered her rightful position as ruler of Scotland. Despite having been implicated in the murder of her husband and having married his killer, she still considered herself queen. Her loyal warden, Anthony Babington, Earl of Shrewsbury, devised a plot to kill Elizabeth, thereby restoring Mary to power and opening the way to the English throne. But the Babington Plot, as it was known, quickly surfaced. Unamused, Elizabeth tightened Mary's security and removed any access to the outside world. She was ordered to stand trial for treason.

This placed James in an untenable position. His mother's action had infuriated Elizabeth, and he was rightfully afraid her fury would extend to him. Elizabeth had good reason to be wary. Many Scots—Catholics in particular—still adored their Queen Mary, whom they viewed as a martyr of English suppression. James could not denounce the mother he'd never known for fear of offending his people. Nor could he fully support her lest he incurred the wrath of Queen Elizabeth. He settled for writing to England with a plea of mercy for Mary, but the appeal was lukewarm.

James did his best to create a safe distance between himself and Mary, the women who may have had his own father killed. He dispatched two commoners, Sir Melville and Master Grey, to plead for the deposed queen. While the two men urged Elizabeth to spare Mary's life, James secretly wrote to the Earl of Essex, one of Elizabeth's favorites, indicating that he no longer had any ties to his mother. It was a dangerous game of cat and mouse.

It was also a game in which Elizabeth had no rival. While she was polite to the Scottish emissaries, she refused to reveal her plans for Mary. Ever a brilliant diplomat, she told the Scots nothing. They couldn't even learn whether Mary was alive or dead. By February 1587, Melville and Grey were back in Scotland having accomplished little more than to irritate the queen of England. The very morning the men were giving their report to the Scottish Council, Mary, Queen of Scots, was being beheaded at Fotheringhay Castle. Elizabeth claimed she didn't want to kill her cousin and fellow monarch. But the Catholic threat was growing. The Protestant queen felt she had no other choice.

Understandably, Mary's execution caused a great deal of tension between England and Scotland. The actual beheading had been bloody and gruesome; the first blow apparently failed to sever her neck. Upon hearing the details, James appeared shaken, but he remained silent. In England, Elizabeth attempted to justify her actions by writing to James that she'd never really intended to cause Mary death. Her people had acted of their own volition. If James didn't denounce Mary's execution, Scotland would be in an uproar. If he did denounce, he risked alienating the English queen. Caught between opposing forces stronger than him, James decided to go hunting.

Tensions only mounted as border skirmishes increased. Rumor had it that James was accepting monies from Catholic Spain. Certain Catholic lords considered this the perfect time to attempt to convert James to their faith. Further south, England was bracing itself for a battle against the Spanish Armada.

The English defeated the Armada in 1588 with an ease that must have surprised even them. However, letters to the king of Spain from two Catholic lords, Huntley and Errol, were intercepted and brought to Elizabeth's attention. These letters begged for Spanish help to invade England. The queen was not happy. James made only a token effort to punish his friend Huntley, but eventually set him free. This was seen as an unwise move, and James' popularity in Scotland began to waver. That was fine with the king. He would soon have other matters to worry about.

Chapter Three

James' Bride and the Witch Hunt

"He has given himself over altogether to the hand of Satan."

—The Privy Council regarding the Earl of Bothwell

At the age of 23, James was considered beyond the age where a king could remain unmarried. Producing an heir was paramount for any monarch, but James had been spending his time with his male favorites instead. Women were not a large part of his life.

There was, of course, no lack of bridal candidates. Since some still considered him a potential convert to Catholicism, a papal niece and a Spanish princess were lined up for consideration. More realistic brides were from Navarre and Denmark, both very Protestant. Catherine, sister of Henry of Navarre (a fierce Protestant and future Catholic convert King Henry IV of France), and Anne, daughter of the king of Denmark, proved to be the top choices.

Discussions were started with both courts. However, at 31 years old, Catherine was considered middle-aged; or, as one courtier put it, "old, cracked, and something worse." Negotiations with Denmark proved more successful, and a marriage by proxy with 14-year-old Anne was arranged. For her, this was considered an advantageous marriage. The young Anne prepared to cross the Channel to a new life as queen of Scotland.

An excited Scottish citizenry prepared for the official royal wedding. After three months, however, there was no sign of the new queen. Word came back from the mainland that storms had made the crossing of Danish ships impossible. By late October 1589, winter gales were causing one accident after another. Two ships in the royal flotilla even crashed into each other. Sea travel was getting too dangerous for the upcoming winter months. The new bride would have to remain at home until spring. Surprisingly, James began to behave like a lovelorn adolescent. He expressed his dismay in poetry, writing, "Oh, cruel Cupid what a ruthless rage."

Then, James decided to travel to Denmark himself to be with his bride. The king wasn't known for his ardor toward women, so this was strange behavior indeed. In an unguarded letter, he presented the reason himself. There was no mention of love or passion for Anne. He was decrying the questions relating to his masculinity, especially in view of his association with male favorites. James was on a quest to prove his manhood. There might have been a second reason. The political situation was heating up in Scotland; James might well have hoped that leaving would help him avoid the worst of it.

Following three weeks of stormy weather, James and his ships landed in Oslo, Norway, where the king finally met his bride in mid-November. The royal couple and their entourage traveled through Sweden to Denmark. By January 21, 1590, James entered Elsinore, Anne's home, to finally meet his in-laws. They remained there until March. Instead of returning to Scotland, James now embarked on a tour of Denmark, including the splendid Royal Academy and the University of Copenhagen. He was obviously in no hurry to return home. Back in Scotland, his Chancellor Maitland was seething over the cost of this trip.

The couple finally arrived on Scottish soil on May 1. James had been absent for six months. They settled at Holyrood Castle with much fanfare. Most of Scotland was thrilled with their lovely new queen. But not all. The moment James returned home, the Kirk voiced its displeasure at a planned Sunday coronation ceremony because Sunday celebrations were unlawful and popish. James did get his way, but once again, the presence of the Kirk served as a frustrating reminder that he wasn't in absolute charge.

Anne settled well into Edinburgh and was made to feel comfortable. Once the excitement of having a new queen abated, questions about Anne's inability to sail the Channel in September were raised. What had deterred her journey? Blame was quickly placed on Copenhagen's governor, Christoffer Valkendorff, who was accused of maintaining a substandard fleet. Certainly, the rough gales were at fault, but Valkendorff pointed out that not all gales are natural. Some are the result of witchcraft.

Sixteenth-century Europe had an obsession with witches. Wicked hags were seen and suspected everywhere. Natural disasters were frequently blamed on witchcraft. In Copenhagen, a supposed witch was put on trial for causing the storms. She confessed to deliberately delaying Anne's fleet. She also named many accomplices, all of whom received the death sentence.

James had always had a lively interest in religion. Now, he began examining the nature of witchcraft in Scotland. Within six months, hundreds of women had been rounded up and accused of an assortment of wrongdoing, including causing great storms. Over a hundred of the women brought to trial were executed for working with the Devil. James watched the trials with fascination. Witchcraft was evil enough, but these women had thwarted his goals and had stood in the way of his marriage. The king of Scotland became so enrapt with the subject that he decided to write a scholarly paper for a wider audience. His treatise was called *Daemonologie*. The writing only fueled Scotland's witch hunts. Across the country, women were accused of evil and summarily executed.

It was a time of turmoil, and the various clan factions took every advantage of the disarray growing in the country. Several Catholic lords, among them the new Earl of Bothwell, Francis Stewart, stormed Holyrood House one day in an attempt to seize or kill James. Fortunately, they were quickly repelled by James' men. One of the witches suspected of causing the storms that delayed Anne's ship, Agnes Sampson, testified that Bothwell was acting on orders of the Devil.

Then, when another set of letters from Scottish lords to Spain were found, the threat of Catholicism grew—as did the rumors against James. It was whispered that James was actually Mary's secretary Rizzio's son and that his marriage had not been consummated because of his preference for young men. While the clans continued fighting each other, the Kirk issued another declaration against James. He was encouraging witchcraft and worse evil; he was harboring Catholics!

Clearly, James was slowly losing control of Scotland. This did not go unnoticed by Queen Elizabeth down south. If James couldn't manage Scotland, how was he supposed to rule England?

1594 began as a good year for James. He had married to prove his virility, and on February 19, 1594, Anne gave birth to an heir to the throne, Prince Henry. The birth was much celebrated. Henry was the first Protestant heir to be born to the throne of Scotland, and that purity had to be strictly maintained. A few days after his birth, James gave custody of his newborn son to his old friend, the Earl of Mar, to be raised in the Mar household. A desperate Anne pleaded with James for custody, but he refused. The Earl of Mar was an undisputed Protestant, while Anne was showing signs of civility to Catholic friends that was being noticed by the Kirk. James would take no risks.

Henry's removal from the household caused a rift between the couple that never really healed. Caught between pleasing his wife and the Kirk, James chose the Kirk. The truth was, now that his manhood had been established, he lost interest in Anne. But the Kirk still had their doubts about James. When they called a meeting of the General Assembly without James' permission, he disputed their right to do so. One of the Kirk ministers, James Melville, angrily informed James, "There are two kings and two kingdoms in Scotland: there is Jesus Christ, the king of the church, whose subject King James VI is, and of whose kingdom he is not a king, nor a lord, nor a head, but a member!" The Kirk was making it clear that they were in charge of Scotland; James was merely along for the ride.

Chapter Four

The Mystery of the Gowrie Plot

"It is a great comfort to think that, at the Day of Judgment, we shall know the whole truth about the Gowrie Conspiracy at last."

—Anonymous Scottish lady

What has become known as the Gowrie Conspiracy is still cloaked in mystery. The incident, however, reveals the turmoil which existed between the various Scottish clans and how James was caught up in the debacle. It also makes clear the lengths to which the Kirk would go to discredit James.

The details that are known indicate that on August 5, 1600, James went on an early hunt near Falkland Palace. He was accompanied by the Duke of Lennox, the Earl of Mar, and the Earl of Kellie. The group was approached by Alexander Ruthven, the brother of John Ruthven, the Earl of Gowrie. According to Alexander, his brother John was holding a foreigner in possession of a great sum of money at their home, Gowrie House. He asked James to talk to the foreigner and determine his intentions and the source of all this wealth. He stressed the importance of complete secrecy.

James and ten of his men arrived at Gowrie House in the afternoon. No preparations had been made for the king's arrival, an unprecedented situation. After being given a hastily prepared meal, James followed Alexander to the second floor, where he expected to find the mysterious foreigner. Instead, he was instantly accosted by Alexander and a servant. Threatening the king with his dagger, Alexander said James must remain silent and left the king in the care of the servant, locking them both in the room. John Ruthven, in the meantime, told James' men that James had left and that they should follow him. His men, however, had seen their king through a window struggling with Alexander and immediately entered the house and ran upstairs and attempted to ram down the locked door. Upon entry, they managed to kill Alexander, and his brother John was also killed in the melee.

The mystery of what happened has three possible explanations: First, the Ruthven brothers were plotting to murder or kidnap King James and lured him to Gowrie House for that purpose. Second, James' arrival at the Gowrie House was a surprise to the brothers, and in reality, James had planned to kill the brothers. Third, an unpremeditated fight broke out as the result of an argument between one of the brothers and the king.

Kidnappings were not a rarity in Scotland at that time. The Ruthven brothers had taken part in several such acts. With relations between England and Scotland tenser than usual, the Earl of Gowrie was seen as a strong supporter of Queen Elizabeth. With the Kirk at odds with James, the church was viewing John Ruthven as a possible new leader and candidate to the English throne. Additionally, the Ruthven brothers' father, William Ruthven, had been executed for high treason during James' early reign. This would certainly give them motive to remove James.

While the facts remain murky, the Kirk's enmity toward James is extremely clear. Even his own lords were conspiring to kill him. And the Earl of Gowrie was, after all, a leader of the Kirks.

The incident was investigated, and reports were sent to Queen Elizabeth. James voluntarily permitted himself to be questioned by members of the Kirk. Such were the Kirk's powers and James' fragile grip as head of state that he was unable to refuse. The Kirk concluded that it had been James' intent to kill the Gowries. It didn't help matters that James happened to owe the brothers a great deal of money. It was the Privy Council that subsequently decided to believe James' version of events—that the Gowries had plotted against him.

The entire plot made it clear that Kirk would never let James rule in peace. In addition, he lacked the needed support of his lords to rule effectively. From the south, Queen Elizabeth watched with exasperation. The future of her beloved country was at stake.

Chapter Five

Taking over Elizabethan England

"I know I have the body but of a weak and feeble woman; but I have the heart and stomach of a king, and of a king of England too."

—Elizabeth I

James' future as king of England was still far from certain with Tudor heirs still lurking in the background. However, they were too far removed from power to make a bold claim to the crown.

James, on the other hand, did hold one trump card: his son, Henry. Henry was growing into a handsome and intelligent young man, utterly adored by his people. In Henry, the Scots, and perhaps the English, saw their bright future. Most importantly, Henry was able to connect with people, a skill James never acquired or even cared about. When the young prince was paraded through the streets of Sterling or Edinburgh, he was wildly cheered by the masses. His physical prowess and love of hunting, jousting, and fencing painted the perfect picture of the ideal royal as opposed to his father, who at this point was physically frail and preferred to spend his time with books. In addition, Henry was considered a pure Protestant, as opposed to James who had been born to Catholic parents. Henry's star rose just as James' popularity was at its lowest.

When James was with his son during outings, he was more of an accompaniment to the boy than the king of the country. James loved his son, but he began to resent the boy's popularity. His dreams of becoming king of England were now linked to the son who easily outshone him.

Still, Henry was the tie to James' goals. In the late 1590s, the scholarly James began working on a book of royal instructions specifically dedicated to his son. The book, named *Basilikon Doron*, provided guidelines on how to rule according to the scripture. It blasted the Kirk, whom he described as "clogged by their own passion." He blamed the hated Kirk on the failure of the Reformation movement to make more progress. As James repeatedly lamented, the Kirk was responsible for all of the ills that the king had to endure. *Basilikon Doron* was widely criticized upon its publication. Once again, James had managed to divide his own country further. It was, however, a runaway bestseller, selling more than 16,000 copies.

Since the Kirk didn't hesitate to criticize the Church of England, *Basilikon Doron* was also sending a subtle message to England. But England was divided as well. An English lawyer named James Dalton raged in front of Parliament that he trusted never to see the day "that ever any Scot or stranger shall have any interest in the Crown of this realm." The point was made. James was a Scot, and thus a foreigner.

For once, James used diplomatic tactics. He engaged in lengthy correspondence with the Earl of Essex, Queen Elizabeth's particular favorite at the time. But many felt that Essex himself had an eye on the throne. In the summer of 1599, he rode into Ireland at the head of the queen's army. This did not sit well with the fickle queen, who would never accept any action that did not meet her expressed approval. Essex was removed from office and placed under arrest. He was eventually executed for treason. James had lost a potentially strong ally at Her Majesty's court. For her part, Elizabeth had lost a potential successor.

During the last years of her life, Elizabeth's tone toward James became more conciliatory. She even raised his pension to 5,000 pounds a year. Meanwhile, James initiated correspondence with Elizabeth's trusted secretary, Sir Robert Cecil. Cecil, who had been Essex's rival for the queen's attention, was receptive to dialogue. Thus began another series of correspondence, this time very secretly. Neither man could be certain how future winds would blow. Caution was a dire necessity. The wily Cecil suggested that James quietly build a support system in England. James argued he was not going behind the queen's back and that he deserved the throne on merit. Much paranoia and secrecy began to surround the English succession. Perhaps for the lack of anyone else, Cecil continued to support James. All that was now necessary was for Queen Elizabeth to die.

The culmination of James' ambitions happened on March 24, 1603. Elizabeth was dead. By unanimous consent, or perhaps by default, James was immediately proclaimed King James I of England and Ireland.

Chapter Six

King James Bible

"There is no difference between London and Edinburgh . . . my course must be between both, to establish peace, and religion, and wealth between the countries."

—James I and VI

James had finally won his coveted prize. One can only imagine his elation. His first step upon becoming king of England and Ireland was to reassure his Scottish subjects. In Edinburgh, he declared that he was still their king. England and Scotland were now one people, one realm, joined together on the same island. They were forever entwined by the will of God, and God had declared him king of a united country. By moving to England, he would not forget or abandon the Scots, but only further their interests.

The decision was made for England's new royal family to stagger its arrival in London. James would go first, to be joined by Anne and their youngest children, Prince Charles and Princess Elizabeth, at a later time. Prince Henry would remain at Sterling Castle in Scotland for the time being.

James' travel to England took over a month. One reason was that he didn't want to enter a London still in mourning. The second reason for the long trek was that he stopped at many towns along the way, exulting in the feasts, fireworks, and adulation he received. Warming to his new role, he pardoned prisoners along the way and handed out knighthoods to Scottish lords in abundance. Some considered this generosity a bribe to protect him against any possible English ill will. But, undoubtedly, James was in a benevolent mood. James' entry into London was a major triumph. All the citizenry flocked to the streets in their finery to welcome their new king. His first address to the Parliament was received very favorably, although a few commented on his "foreign" accent.

Back in Scotland, Anne moved to Sterling Castle to see her son Henry for the first time in years. A battle ensued between Lord Mar and Queen Anne over custody of nine-year-old Henry. James had been very explicit in his instructions. Even in the case of the king's death, Henry was to remain with Mar. Anne, with her Catholic friends, was to be barred from any access.

Thus, Anne gathered a group of likeminded lords in an attempt to take her oldest son. When James learned of her actions, he ordered her attendance in London immediately. Anne continued her fight. Finally, Lord Mar handed Henry over to the Council, and the Council handed Henry to Anne. This argument was just another example of James digging in his heels needlessly rather than offering a compromise. Together, Anne and Henry made their way to London. Upon her arrival, James, Anne, and Henry rode through the city, providing the citizens with its first look of their new king, queen, and prince. They were pleased with what they saw.

For obvious reasons, the English Privy Council was concerned over any possible changes James might make. To their great surprise and relief, James kept the status quo, making no changes in personnel. He even kept the all-powerful Sir Cecil. Scottish lords were kept from any important English positions. It all looked like a successful transfer of power. James had managed to keep all of his subjects satisfied. Still, things were not what they seemed.

Since the reign of Henry VIII, the power of the king's (or queen's) intimates had shifted from the Privy Council to the Royal Bedchamber. The private lodgings of the monarch had slowly become the true seat of influence. While the plan was to staff the Bedchamber with an equal number of Scots and English, James managed to surround himself with close courtiers that were all Scottish. All important positions within the household were now held by Scots. This new schism and monopoly of the king's person immediately brought complaints from the English, but to no avail. James simply avoided the Privy Council whenever possible and went riding with his Scottish coterie when they complained too loudly. This he did not consider a dereliction of royal duties. During his reign in Scotland, he had spent years avoiding any direct confrontation with those in power.

England, however, was not Scotland. For 44 years, Elizabeth had made herself the center of attention, basking in the admiration of everyone around her. She had loved being surrounded by her courtiers and knew well how to play them against each other to get her way. The new king's seeming indifference did not go over well. When questioned, James replied that the fresh air during hunts was more suited to his health than the air in London. During his absence, he simply approved any of the Council's actions, in effect placing them in charge.

To James, this was a perfect balance. To the Council, unsure of its exact limitations and power, it became a time of frustration while trying to track down the king. The Council members weren't the only ones who were annoyed. The owners of the properties through which James rode to hunt and whose crops and gardens he destroyed were displeased as well. The honeymoon period was coming to a quick end.

James remained not only aloof from his Council, but he also drifted from his family. Anne set up her own household at Greenwich House. There, she hosted glittering masks and salons, where both Protestants and Catholics were welcomed. She surrounded herself with writers such as Ben Jonson and John Donne. James, on the other hand, scorned art and science and fell asleep during plays. During this seventeenth-century Renaissance, James remained a sixteenth-century ruler oblivious to a changing world. Once again, now at the age of 13, Prince Henry soared in popularity. While England had once looked toward a future with James, their eyes and hopes were directed at his heir.

Unlike the Scottish Kirk, the Church of England had its basis in the divine rights of kings. Here, James was head of the church. Still, there were factions within the church, with the Calvinists and Puritans insisting their rights were being infringed. James called a meeting of the Church of England's bishops and Puritan leaders at Hampton Court. He relished few things more than a good religious debate, and here he was in charge. The bishops were impressed with his knowledge; the Puritans less so.

Like the Kirk, they quibbled over every nuance and word. The centuries-old wedding vow, "with my body I thee worship," was considered too sexual, and the Puritans demanded the phrase be struck. Finally in charge of ecclesiastical matters, James was more amused than angry and simply ignored them, something that had been impossible with the Kirk. The bishops united behind their king, strengthening the powers of the Church of England, much to the chagrin of any remaining Catholics who had been promised religious freedom. As for the Puritans, they were left with no choice but to seek another place to worship as they saw fit.

The approval of the bishops was a huge revelation to James. All of his life, he'd been forced to appease the hated

Kirk. Now, he made the rules and had the Church of England's firm approval. This success encouraged him to continue his interest in religion. He ordered a new translation of the Bible into English and commissioned 54 translators for the job. These translators worked as a team, with other teams checking the translations. The feat took seven years, but the King James Bible was the result. It is still in use today.

Chapter Seven

The Gunpowder Plot

"Remember, remember the 5th of November, the gunpowder treason and plot. I know for no reason that the gunpowder treason should ever be forgot."

—British nursery rhyme

While it is uncertain whether there was actually a plot against James during the Gowrie Conspiracy, there can be no such doubt about the Gunpowder Plot. Catholic plotters were determined to kill the king, his family, and take a good many members of Parliament with them. But what exactly caused this bitterness among the Catholics?

Starting in the Tudor era, Catholics were banned from attending Mass and were heavily fined if they broke that law. James' arrival in England had filled them with hope. It was rumored that he was tolerant of Catholics and that his wife surrounded herself with Catholic friends. The Catholics had high expectations of James and were greatly encouraged by his arrival. The new king gave important posts to several Catholic sympathizers. Things were looking up.

However, the meeting of religious leaders at Hampton Court quickly squashed their hopes. James' bond with the Church of England had strengthened the ties between the monarchy and the church, while Catholics were again being fined for illegal worship. Most Catholics were willing to pay the fines and pray in secrecy. But not all.

Blessed with an abundance of personal charm and magnetism, Robert Catesby was a fervent Catholic who refused to take the required Protestant Oath of Supremacy. With his hopes on the king shattered, Catesby recruited like-minded Catholics into his conspiracy. The plan was a marvel of simplicity: they were to blow up the House of the Lords during the State Opening of the Parliament.

Catesby, along with several friends, including Guy Fawkes, was in charge of organizing the plot. Fawkes, a devout Catholic who had served in the Spanish army, was ready to take a stand against the Reformation. The group, which quickly grew to 13 men, rented a house in Westminster, and Guy Fawkes lived there as the caretaker, calling himself John Johnson. Fawkes' assignment was to light the gunpowder, blow up the Parliament while in session, kill as many people as possible, and flee to Europe. The rented house was conveniently located near a cellar directly beneath the House of Lords. Over a period of several months, 36 barrels of gunpowder were moved to the secret cellar.

The plotters were planning more than mass destruction. With the king dead (so they hoped), the plot included the installation of James' young daughter, Princess Elizabeth, to the throne as their very own puppet queen. They would settle for nothing less than full restoration of Catholicism in England.

On October 26, 1605, Lord Monteagle received an anonymous letter telling him to not to come to the opening of Parliament. A servant of Monteagle managed to warn the plotters that they had been discovered. Yet the plotters were determined to continue with their plan. Too much was at stake for them to quit now.

Soon after the discovery of the letter, a full-blown search of the Houses of Parliament took place. The barrels of gunpowder were found under a huge heap of firewood;

Fawkes, who was in the vicinity, was promptly arrested. While London rejoiced in the plot's discovery, "John Johnson," who refused to give his real name of Guy Fawkes, was interrogated. Fawkes said nothing. Frustrated by his silence, James allowed the interrogators to use torture.

The remaining conspirators scattered, some fleeing for safety, some scrambling to gather men and weapons for an armed uprising. By November 8, the main group was caught. The confrontation was quick. Several men died, three were captured. Five plotters escaped, but they were eventually captured. All were found guilty, including Guy Fawkes, and executed.

The repercussions for the innocent and ordinary Catholic population were immense. Laws were quickly passed to keep Catholics from practicing law and serving in England's army or navy. They lost their right to vote. Their reputation was irretrievably tarnished and would remain so until the next century. They were even blamed for catastrophes such as the Great Fire of London. Catholics didn't get their voting rights back until the turn of the eighteenth century. English Catholics were now forced to take an oath of allegiance to the crown and deny the power of the Pope. Needless to say, the new infringement of rights against Catholics did not sit well with the Pope. Once again, James found himself embroiled in religious controversy.

Today, the discovery of the Gunpowder Plot is celebrated each year on Guy Fawkes Day on November 5. Effigies of Fawkes are dragged through the streets. Great fireworks are included in the celebration, a reminder of the fireworks that might have happened had the plot succeeded.

Chapter Eight

The King's Favorite Men

*"You may be sure that I love the Earl of Buckingham more
than anyone else, and more than you who are here
assembled. I wish to speak in my own behalf and not to
have it thought to be a defect, for Jesus Christ did the same,
and therefore I cannot be blamed. Christ had John, and I
have George."*

—James I and VI

James' sexual preference had always been a source of
rumors. Although he was fond of his wife, Anne, the two
lacked any kind of a bond that would keep them close. By
1607, the pretense was pretty much over. The queen had
given birth to seven children at this point, three of whom
would survive to adulthood. After the birth and death of
their final child, Sophia, in June 1607, the couple rarely
spent time under the same roof.

Instead, James found a new favorite in court. Scotsman
Robert Carr was a handsome 21-year-old when he first
appeared at the court of James I in 1607. James was quickly
smitten. Carr was named Gentleman of the Bedchamber, a
position that guaranteed him easy access to the king. James
bestowed many favors on the young man, much to the
disgust of the entire court. By 1614, Carr had been named
Earl of Somerset as well as Lord Chamberlain. He was
given properties, acted as James' secretary, and was then
promoted to Viscount Rochester. This made him the first
Scot with a seat in the House of Lords. The Parliament has

always been wary of Scottish power at the English court, and this alienated them even more.

At some point, Carr fell in love with the wife of the Earl of Essex, Frances Howard. Such confusing situations were not rare for the times. Apparently, Lord Essex was impotent, and Carr happily filled his place. James agreed with Carr that the Essexes should get an annulment, which would pave the way for Carr and Frances to marry. Sir Thomas Overbury, Carr's close friend and advisor, warned against such a move. The powerful Howards were very much in favor of it. It was as if James could not exist without being between disagreeing factions.

Carr and Frances did marry. However, Frances never forgave Overbury for speaking out against the union. When Overbury died of poisoning, both Carr and Frances were suspected. Frances confessed; Carr did not. They were both found guilty in 1615 and imprisoned.

Without Carr at his side, James' eye wandered toward a new favorite. This man would be George Villiers, who at the age of 21 was already famous for his graceful manner, long, lean legs, and good looks. Those courtiers and lords who had opposed Carr encouraged James' new interest. The royal court provided Villiers with an entirely new and glamorous wardrobe with which to please the king. He was made royal cupbearer, keeping him in close contact with James.

Villiers rose quickly through the ranks, from Gentleman of the Bedchamber to Master of Horse, Viscount, then Duke of Buckingham and Lord Admiral of the Fleet. He was the highest-ranking member of the court who was not a member of the royal family. In 1617, James felt the need to explain Villiers' rapid rise to the lords, saying, "I act like a man, and confess to loving those dear to me more than other men. You may be sure that I love the Earl of

Buckingham more than anyone else." James not only elevated Villiers in rank, but his entire family as well.

Through Villiers' influence, Francis Bacon, an English philosopher and statesman, was named Lord Chancellor. James was more than happy to comply as Bacon supported the royal prerogative over Parliament. James knew he could count on Bacon when he needed to proclaim his God-given rights as king. However, clearly not accepting James' royal prerogatives, Parliament had Francis Bacon impeached for bribery.

Parliament also objected to Villiers' increasing involvement in the decision making. Villiers was a supporter of Catholic Spain, which added to Parliament's ire. He supported a union between Prince Charles and the Spanish Infanta, Maria Anna—a match which many Protestants feared.

As Villiers' powers grew, he reached across the northern border and became involved in Irish affairs as well. Parliament was eager to call an investigation into these questionable acts. Slyly, Villiers instigated a conflict between King James and Parliament over the potential Spanish betrothal. This forced yet another dissolution of Parliament. James' prerogatives were to become a major issue between the king and the English Parliament.

While James' popularity waned, Prince Henry was invested as prince of Wales. He was a popular young man and showed great leadership potential. However, James was hit with another blow when his young heir died of typhoid at the age of 18, immediately raising his second son, Charles, as the heir to the throne. Few heirs were mourned by the English public as widely as Henry. James, who is said to have disliked funerals, did not attend his son's.

Chapter Nine

The Divine Rights of Kings

"Kings are justly called gods, for that they exercise a manner or resemblance of divine power upon earth."

—James I and VI

James found himself continuously at odds with the Parliament of England. His views on Parliament were derived from Scottish laws, where the Kirk may argue with him, but where the Civil Council followed his bidding. The independence of the English Parliament turned into a new thorn in his side. Members of Parliament felt free to disagree with the king's policies, leading to considerable friction between them.

James believed that as king, his rights were God-given. His books, *The True Law of Free Monarchies* and *Basilikon Doron*, described his ideas on the subject. Parliament begged to differ. It viewed their relationship on an equal footing. As James told his son Henry, "Hold no Parliaments but for the necessity of new laws, which would be but seldom."

James was eager to unite Scotland and England as one realm and one parliament—with him, of course, as the one monarch. He wanted to be known as the king of Great Britain. The Parliament turned down his request. James, however, defied Parliament and took the title by proclamation.

As James popularity waned, his debts mounted. As king of Scotland, he had not been accountable for his expenditures. The fact was, he was financially irresponsible, spending grandly on himself and his courtiers and favorites. In 1610, the Earl of Salisbury had proposed what was called the Great Contract to the House of Commons in an attempt to limit the king's spending. Under this Contract, Parliament would provide James with £600,000 to pay off his debts. In return, the king would give up certain royal concessions, such as the right of wardship. (The king could be named as ward to a minor and come into possession of the minor's property.)

James' answer was to dissolve Parliament. He never bothered to consider the proposal. This left him in dire needs of funds. As a potential solution, a match was proposed by Catholic ministers between the heir to the throne, Charles, and the Spanish Infanta, Maria Anna. An affiliation with powerful Spain could prove profitable. Protestant ministers, however, argued assiduously against such a match. Charles' sister, Elizabeth, in the meantime, became engaged to Frederick, the son of Frederick IV, Count of Palatine. Frederick was head of the Protestant Union, and it was seen as a good match.

Still, James needed money. The only way to acquire funds was to reinstate Parliament, which he was loath to do. Having no other choice, he reconvened Parliament in April of 1614. His plea for money was ensconced in a long, rambling speech. First, in an effort to gain Protestant support, he called for greater enforcement of laws against recalcitrant Catholics. Second, he pointed out that the marriage of his daughter had been to a Protestant, a tremendous benefit to the country, and the wedding had been expensive. He needed reimbursement. Despite his pleas and desperate need for funds, James was unwilling to make his own concessions to Parliament. The meetings proved fruitless. Once again, James dissolved Parliament.

Since the match between Charles and Maria Anna didn't work out, James entered secret discussions with France to have Charles marry one of King Louis XIII's sisters. France, of course, was another Catholic country. While discussions continued with France, James also, secretly, revived negotiations with Spain for the Infanta. James' talent for brewing trouble appeared endless.

On the continent, Catholics and Protestants were engaging in more fierce battles than ever. When the Holy Roman Empire and the Protestant Bohemians engaged in conflict during the late 1610s, Frederick V, James' son-in-law, was named king of Bohemia. Although Frederick ruled only briefly, this triggered one of the worst religious wars in Europe, the Thirty Years' War, a three-decade battle between Europe's Protestants and Catholics. Hundreds of thousands of people died for a God no-one could agree upon.

James reinstated Parliament in 1621 to vote on funds to help his son-in-law, who was soon deposed from the Bohemian throne. The House of Commons refused to provide adequate funds. On the other hand, it voted that England should go to war against Catholic Spain. Specific in the Commons' demands was a Protestant marriage for Prince Charles and greater enforcement of laws against Catholics. James considered his son's marriage a royal prerogative and told the Commons to cease interference with what he considered a personal matter. The House of Commons insisted on being able to enforce its rights. In November of 1621, James dissolved Parliament for the third time.

In direct conflict with the wishes of the Commons, James turned to Catholic Spain for help in restoring Elizabeth and Frederick to their throne. Prince Charles, now 23 years old, traveled to Spain in hopes of receiving the hand of the Infanta in marriage. It was a rash move.

Charles was risking official disapproval, not knowing if the Infanta Maria Anna would even consider marrying a non-Catholic. Charles returned to England without the Infanta and without support from Spain. Obviously as impetuous as his father, Charles now went after a French match and called for war against the Catholic Hapsburgs.

The anti-Catholic sentiments in Parliament were strong. There was a chance that there would be an agreement to finance a war against Spain. Negotiations remained ambiguous. Whose side England was on in this disastrous European religious war was anyone's guess. James wanted peace with Spain. It was Charles, his heir, who resented the lack of parliamentary support for the war—a mindset which would influence his own reign and bring about deadly results.

Chapter Ten

James I, the Peacemaker

"I will tell thee, man, what is obedience."

—James I and VI

When James left Scotland to become king of England in 1603, he had assured his Scottish subjects that he would still be their king, only on a larger scale. As he repeatedly promised, England and Scotland were now one country, both equally dear to his heart. In reality, James had not visited Scotland for 13 years. In effect, the Privy Council had full power to act according to its wishes. The mail system between the two countries assured that James merely rubber-stamped any of the Privy Council's actions. Scotland's chief ministers made all important decisions. It was a haphazard rule by an absentee king. It did little to improve relations between England and Scotland. In a way, James' lack of interest in Scotland mirrored that of his mother, Mary, who only wanted the crown of England.

In 1616, James unexpectedly announced that he would visit Scotland. The Scottish Privy Council immediately began sprucing up the country, especially the castles which had fallen into some neglect during James' long absence. Accommodations had to be made for James' retinue of 5,000 men, who were about to embark onto the Scottish countryside. Beggars were hidden, the streets were swept, and fine wine was imported from France. Thousands of pheasants and other game were gathered into local forests to enable the visiting king to hunt at his pleasure. Scotland was a poor country when compared to England, but the Scots were determined to impress their absentee monarch. All of these improvements were paid for by an additional tax.

James and his men made their way through Scotland with all due celebrations. But the English and the Scots eyed each other with distrust. They really had no common ground. They were not, as James had promised, "one people." One English soldier called the Scots "the stinking people." The Scots along the roadside looked enviously at the splendid uniforms and clothes of the English.

Some members of the Privy Council wondered what exactly was the purpose of this long-delayed visit. Why had the king chosen this particular time to return to his home country? Especially nervous about the visit was the Kirk. They had long shown their disapproval toward the king. Exactly what were his plans for religion and how was he planning to interfere with their rights as religious leaders? James had clearly not forgotten his enmity toward them. His plans were soon made clear. He attended church services offering English prayers. He kneeled during worship, something far too popish for the Kirk to consider proper. He mandated by law to allow celebrations on Sundays. Sports and other games were also to be allowed on holy days. The Scottish Parliament was left with little choice but to pass James' new laws. James was now 55 years old and must have rejoiced at his final victory over the Kirk.

James was to meet a hard blow, however, when he returned home. His wife, Anne, had wasted away after a long illness in 1619. James had not seen his wife for some time and did not attend her funeral, as he had not attended the funeral of his son, Prince Henry. Her burial had to be postponed due to James' reluctance to provide funds. Perhaps his actions were less callous than they sound. At the time of Anne's death, James became quite ill himself. Immediately, leading bishops and political leaders were summoned to what appeared to be his deathbed. Rather than a show of mourning, James was besieged with questions. Would the Catholics remain under pressure? Would Charles be permitted to marry the Spanish princess, which was his stated desire? The country was still much divided on religious issues and looking to James for answers. Fortunately, James recovered from his illness and escaped the necessity of making firm decisions.

The Thirty Years' War was raging throughout Europe. What had begun as a clash over religion now turned into a fight for dominance. France and Spain especially were vying for leadership. Prince Charles, unhappy about his failure to secure a Spanish marriage, demanded that James declare war on Spain. He had the full support of the powerful George Villiers, once James' constant companion and now Charles' ally. Parliament showed little opposition to such a war. It was, however, something James wanted to avoid. He preferred peace.

James had another health relapse and was kept at Royston. Villiers never left his side and took full control, especially over the king's medical treatment. He ordered special servings of julep prepared for the king's consumption. James' condition only worsened. Accusations were floating around that Villiers was trying to poison the king. Upon inspection, however, no problem was found with his special julep. After a few days, James suffered a severe stroke and died on March 27, 1625.

Charles and Villiers immediately took charge. Charles, now King Charles I, petitioned Parliament for funds for a war against Spain, something that James, the Peacemaker King, had avoided. Charles immediately secured a Catholic marriage with Henrietta Maria, sister of King Louis XIII of France. To add to Parliament's distress, Charles lent seven naval ships to France to aid in their fight against the Protestant Huguenots, while at the same time promising to suppress Catholicism in England.

Charles I turned into one of the most controversial English kings, initiating a deadly civil war between Protestants and Catholics. At the order of Parliament, Charles I was eventually beheaded on January 29, 1649 after a disastrous reign. England was to continue in a state of civil war until the reign of Queen Mary II, James I's great-granddaughter, when a frustrated Parliament asked her husband, William of Orange, to invade England and take over in an effort to stop the bloodbath. They promised him full powers alongside Mary, something that had never happened before or since. England was in dire straits and desperate.

William, later King William III, with the help of the Duke of Marlboro, succeeded in a quick invasion in what was known as the Glorious Revolution. England was finally at peace. The reign of William and Mary at last brought an end to the religious discord in England. The Church of England was declared the official church of the state, and the first steps toward freedom of worship were taken with the passing of the Toleration Act in 1689. The long, bloody reigns of James I's son and grandsons had been brought to an end.

Conclusion

James I, England's first Stuart king, continues to have a reputation as a lazy king who gave too much power to his male favorites. While he attempted to unite England and Scotland, he achieved very little agreement between his two nations, who continued to remain suspicious of each other.

His predecessor, Elizabeth I, had inherited the same religious controversies that James had. Yet Elizabeth was able to maintain a strong command over her subjects and the Parliament, something James was unable, or unwilling, to do. His lack of control was the main cause of many problems during his reign. His inability to satisfy either Protestants or Catholics widened the schism between the two factions.

Still, James was not a bad king. He is best remembered for the translation of the Bible into English, making it accessible to all. During the start of the bloody Thirty Years' War that would engulf Europe, James did his best to keep England out of the turmoil. His descendants, however, brought about a bloody civil war that was to last for several generations. Peace in England was not achieved until the last Stuart king, James II, was dethroned and William III of the House of Hanover together with Mary II finally truly united England in a state of peace.

Made in the USA
Columbia, SC
21 February 2024

32088479R00024